This book belongs to:

_____

CW00953297

A catalogue record for this book is available from the British Library

Published by Ladybird Books Ltd
80 Strand, London, WC2R 0RL
A Penguin Company

2 4 6 8 10 9 7 5 3 1
© LADYBIRD BOOKS LTD MMVIII
LADYBIRD and the device of a Ladybird are trademarks of Ladybird Books Ltd

ISBN: 978-1-84646-935-0

Printed in China

My best book about...

The Sea

Written by Mandy Ross
Illustrated by Liz and Kate Pope

All kinds of creatures swim in the sea.
Point to the ones you like best.

An old shipwreck is lying on the seabed. Can you find the treasure?

Let's go fishing!

Which fisherman has caught a fish?

Watch out! This hungry shark is looking for a meal.

Point to all the little fish,
safe in their hiding places.

Submarines are ships that go under the water.

Look out, Captain! Can you find your way back up to the top?

Oh no! The octopuses have got their tentacles tangled!

Which octopuses are holding hands?
Can you wave your arms like an octopus?

Sea turtles swim very gracefully.
Can you match each one to its pattern?

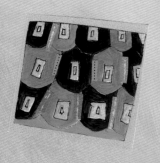

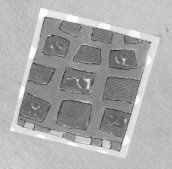

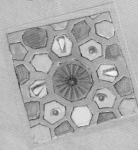

Some fish live among the coral reefs in warm seas.

How many yellow fish can you count?
How many blue ones?

Seahorses like to live in pairs.
They can link their tails together.

Can you find a matching partner for each seahorse?

How many nippy crabs can you count here on the seabed?

Can you nip your claws and scuttle sideways like a crab?

Can you help the baby whale swim through the ocean to his mummy?

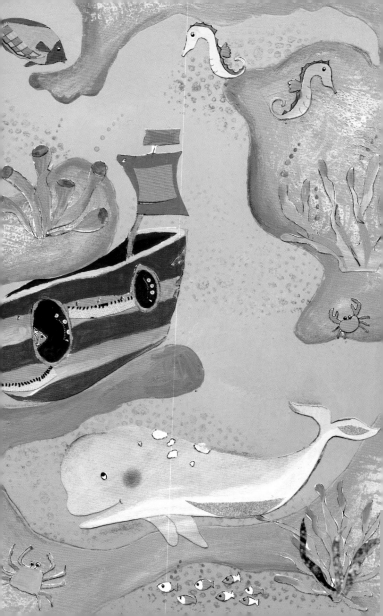

Under the sea is a wonderful place!
Who would you like to meet there?

What would you like to find?